The Eight Beatitudes of Jesus

Blessed are the poor in spirit: for theirs is the kingdom of heaven.

Blessed are they that mourn: for they shall be comforted.

Blessed are the meek: for they shall inherit the earth.

Blessed are they which do hunger and thirst after righteousness: for they shall be filled.

Blessed are the merciful: for they shall obtain mercy.

Blessed are the pure in heart: for they shall see God.

Blessed are the peacemakers: for they shall be called the children of God.

Blessed are they which are persecuted for righteousness' sake: for theirs is the kingdom of heaven.

Matthew 5: 3-10

King James Version (KJV)

The Book Of Alzheimer's

For African American Congregations

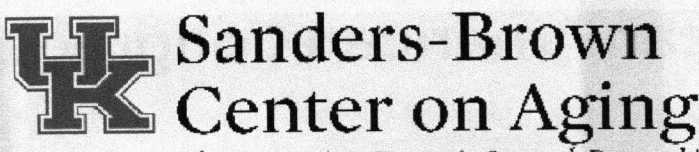

The Balm In Gilead acknowledges the Sanders-Brown Center on Aging at the University of Kentucky as the original developers of The Book of Alzheimer's.

ACKNOWLEDGEMENT

The Book of Alzheimer's for African American Churches and **Memory Sunday** were originally developed by the African American Dementia Outreach Partnership (AADOP) and Outreach and Retention Core of the Alzheimer's Disease Center supported by the National Institute on Aging at the Sanders-Brown Center on Aging at the University of Kentucky. The Sanders-Brown Center on Aging at the University of Kentucky granted permission to The Balm In Gilead to adapt and utilize all materials related to Memory Sunday campaign, including the Book of Alzheimer's for African American Churches. Permission is granted to adapt this initiative, designed as a local initiative in the State of Kentucky, for a national Alzheimer's awareness campaign targeting African Americans across the United States.

The Balm In Gilead wishes to acknowledge the Sanders-Brown Center on Aging at the University of Kentucky as the developers of the original Book of Alzheimer's and the development of Memory Sunday as a local effort in the State of Kentucky. Further, The Balm In Gilead wishes to thank the University of Kentucky, Sanders-Brown Center for its collaborative partnership to support the advancement and fulfillment of mutual goals related to Alzheimer's Disease and cognitive health issues among African Americans. The Balm In Gilead also wishes to thank all persons that contributed to the original guide and all of its success thus far.

As we enter this new season, there are great opportunities for new partnerships and collaborations to increase awareness in the African American community about Alzheimer's disease and other dementias. We wish to acknowledge the Center for Outreach in Alzheimer's Aging and Community Health at the A&T University, the Alzheimer's Association, US Against Alzheimer's, the National Human Genome Center at Howard University, CDC Healthy Brain Initiative and all congregations who are committed to becoming a beacon of light that shines bright for Alzheimer's awareness; compassionate care for those living with the disease; and their caregivers.

The Balm In Gilead's National Brain Health Center for African Americans (NBHCAA), is the new home for The Book of Alzheimer's for African American Congregations, Memory Sunday and all related materials. The NBHCAA is a training institute and online resource center designed to raise awareness of the issues of cognitive health among African Americans by working through existing networks of faith-based health awareness ministries/programs and by establishing new collaborations with research institutions and organizations such as the National Black Nurses Association, National Medical Association, AARP and others.

The Balm In Gilead invites all organizations and individuals who desire to join our efforts to contact us at info@balmingilead.org.

Introduction

The Book of Alzheimer's is a resource guide for congregations serving African Americans who desire to help families and individuals cope with dementia, including Alzheimer's. The burden of dementia is tremendous in African American communities. According to the Alzheimer's Association, African Americans are two to three times more likely than whites to develop dementia. More than 5 million people in the country have Alzheimer's and this number is expected to double by the year 2030. It is now estimated that one out of every nine persons over the age of 65 is living with Alzheimer's and one in three will die from this incurable disease. Unfortunately, data suggests that African Americans entering the age of risk (age 65 and over) will more than double to 6.9 million over the next 30 years.

Alzheimer's is a very serious health challenge for the African American community and we must ACT NOW!

The role of faith communities in addressing Alzheimer's cannot be overstated. For persons living with Alzheimer's and for those who care for them, caring congregations are essential to both the physical and spiritual care one might receive. The Book of Alzheimer's for African American Congregations is designed to share facts about this disease and ideas on how congregations can provide sensitive and appropriate support to families and individuals as they struggle through the process of this currently incurable disease.

The Book of Alzheimer's and the Memory Sunday Tool Kit (free downloads at http://www.brainhealthcenterforafricanamericans.org/memory-sunday-toolkit) are companion, resource guides of congregations participating in Memory Sunday, the 2nd Sunday in June!

Within the pages of The Book of Alzheimer's, you will find:

- The fundamentals of Alzheimer's disease and dementia
- Key descriptions of the impact of Alzheimer's on families as well as African American communities
- How to provide quality care for people with memory loss
- Suggestions for building a support network for persons living with Alzheimer's
- Discussions and activities for compassionate support for caregivers
- Information on understanding why more African Americans must participate in clinical studies

Lela Knox Shanks, a prominent African American leader in Lincoln, Nebraska who cared for her husband with Alzheimer's disease, said, "the best advice to fellow caregivers is to connect faith to everyday life." The Book of Alzheimer's will help members of congregations reach out to caregivers like Lela and let them know that they are traveling the caregiving journey not only with personal faith, but also with a supportive community.

Dr. Pernessa C. Seele
CEO & Founder, The Balm In Gilead, Inc.

Sanders-Brown Center on Aging Staff
University of Kentucky, Lexington, KY

The Serenity Prayer

God grant me the serenity
to accept the things I cannot change;
The courage to change the things I can;
And wisdom to know the difference.

Living one day at a time;
Enjoying one moment at a time;
Accepting hardships as the pathway to peace;

Taking, as He did, this sinful world
as it is, not as I would have it;
Trusting that He will make all things right
if I surrender to His Will;
That I may be reasonably happy in this life
and supremely happy with Him
forever in the next.
Amen.

This non-denominational prayer may be helpful for caregivers and newly diagnosed patients. The message is very appropriate to the challenge of the disease, and repetition of the prayer may reinforce the meaning of the message.

Now faith is the substance of things hoped for,
the evidence of things not seen.

Hebrews 11:1

King James Version (KJV)

Table of Contents

Alzheimer's Disease & Dementia 11
    Overview 12
    Cognitive Health 12
    Understanding Dementia 12
    What is Alzheimer's Disease? 13
    Progression of Alzheimer's 14
    Recognizing the warning signs 15
    List of the most common symptoms: 16
    Diagnosis and Treatment 18
    Reducing the Risk of Alzheimer's 21
    "Six Pillars of Brain Health." 21

Dementia and The African American Community 23
    Overview 24
    Alzheimer's & African Americans – Sobering Facts 24
    Women 25
    Heredity 25
    Role of Pre-existing Health Problems 25
    Socioeconomic Challenges for African Americans with Alzheimer's 26

Caring for a Person with Dementia 29
    Overview 30
    Common Causes of Behavior Changes 30
    Approaches to Responding to Behavior Changes 31
    Communication Challenges 33
    Aggression and Other Behavior Challenges 35
    Sleep Problems are Common 36
    People with Dementia Benefit from Activities 37

A Caregiver's Journey – Taking Care of You Too 44
    Overview 45
    Challenges of being a Caregiver 45
    Stress and The Caregiver 46
    Supporting Caregivers to Plan Ahead 47
    Words of Wisdom for Caregivers 48

Keeping the Faith: Churches Response to Alzheimer's 50
    Overview 51
    Importance of Religion and Faith 51

Importance of Participating in Research and Clinical Studies 56
    Overview 57
    Importance of Participation in Research 57
    Clinical Trials: What Are They? 59
    Lessons from the African American Dementia Outreach Partnership (AADOP): 60

REFERENCES 63

The Lord is my shepherd; I shall not want.
He maketh me to lie down in green pastures: he leadeth me beside the still waters.
He restoreth my soul: he leadeth me in the paths of righteousness for his name's sake.
Yea, though I walk through the valley of the shadow of death, I will fear no evil: for thou art with me; thy rod and thy staff they comfort me.
Thou preparest a table before me in the presence of mine enemies: thou anointest my head with oil; my cup runneth over.
Surely goodness and mercy shall follow me all the days of my life: and I will dwell in the house of the Lord for ever.

Psalm 23
King James Version (KJV)

CHAPTER | 1

Alzheimer's Disease & Dementia

"Alzheimer's disease does not discriminate between rich and poor, African American and white. All individuals touched by this disease deserve our love and the best care available."

William R. Markesbery, MD
Sanders-Brown Center on Aging at the University of Kentucky

Overview

This chapter will discuss the following:

- **What is Cognitive Health?**
- **What is Dementia and Alzheimer's disease?**
- **How to recognize signs & symptoms.**
- **How is it diagnosed & treated.**
- **What can you do to reduce your risk of developing Alzheimer's?**

This chapter is intended to provide faith leaders and other members of the community with the information necessary to have a better understanding of Alzheimer's disease, which is the fourth leading cause of death among African Americans and the sixth leading cause of death in the United States.

Cognitive Health

To better understand dementia and diseases like Alzheimer's, it is important to understand what is cognitive health. Concisely, cognitive health encompasses the physical, mental and emotional brain functions related to how we think, reason and remember.

Cognitive health includes the following brain functions:
- Language
- Attention
- Perception
- Remembered skills (such as driving)
- Thought
- Memory
- Executive function (the ability to plan and carry out tasks)
- Judgment
- Ability to live a purposeful life

As we get older, we move through the cognitive health continuum or cycle. Without the presence of disease or injury to the brain, we should expect to maintain an age appropriate level of cognitive health that allows us to continue performing many of the brain functions listed above. However, when brain function changes, cognitive health begins to decline. Persons may experience what is called Mild Cognitive Impairment or MCI.

Mild Cognitive impairment (MCI) is a slight, but noticeable decline in cognitive abilities. This decrease in function, overtime becomes more noticeable to the individual and others. Identifying MCI is important because persons with MCI have an increased risk of developing Alzheimer's or another type of dementia. Depending on what caused the MCI, it is possible to stop the decline. Memory and thinking may even improve.

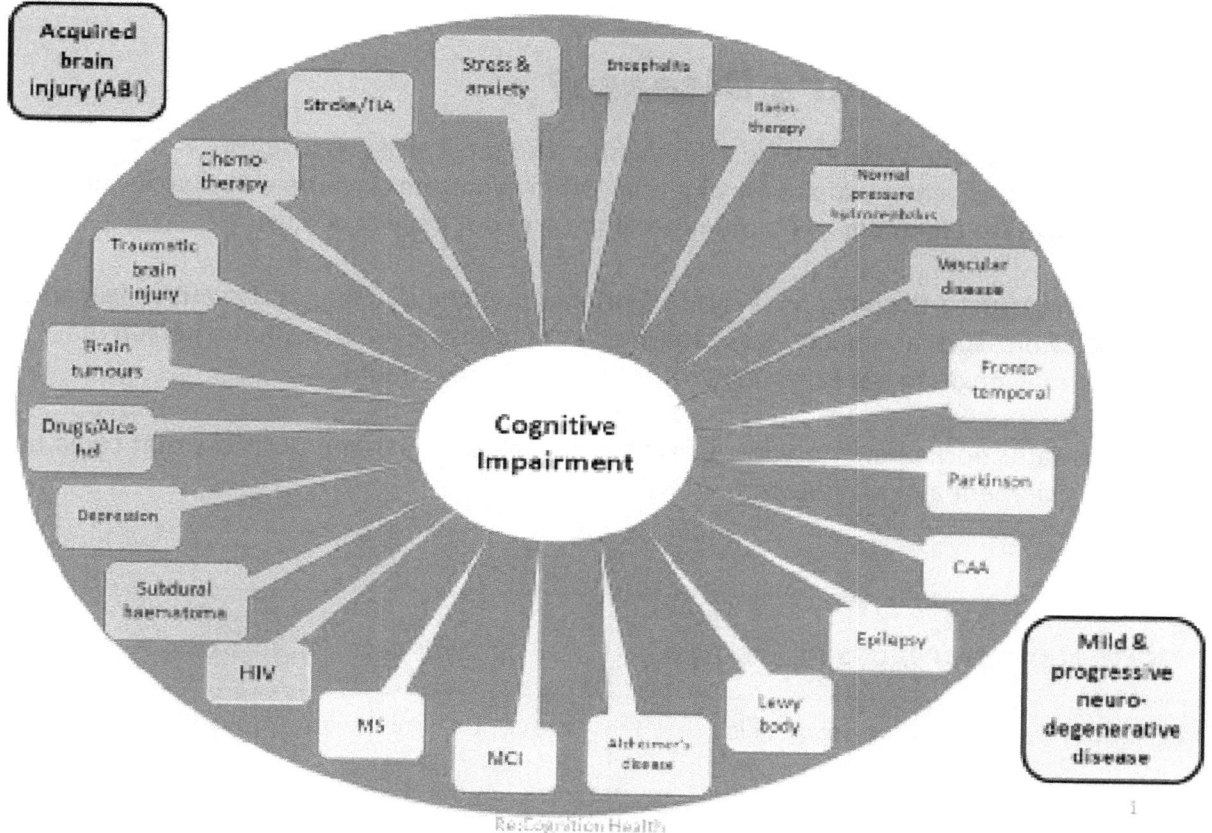

The graphic above illustrates some possible causes of MCI and dementia.

Understanding Dementia

Dementia is a medical condition that affects our memory, thinking and behavior. Dementia is a term that describes the overall decrease in mental ability and it interferes with our daily living activities. Dementia is the result of disease or injury to the brain. The illustration below gives an example of the relationship between dementia, Alzheimer's and other cognitive health problems.

Dementia, sometimes referred to as, "being senile" **is not a normal part of aging**. As we age, we may have some slowing of our cognitive ability, but dementia is a progressive decline in our memory and function that impacts our daily lives.

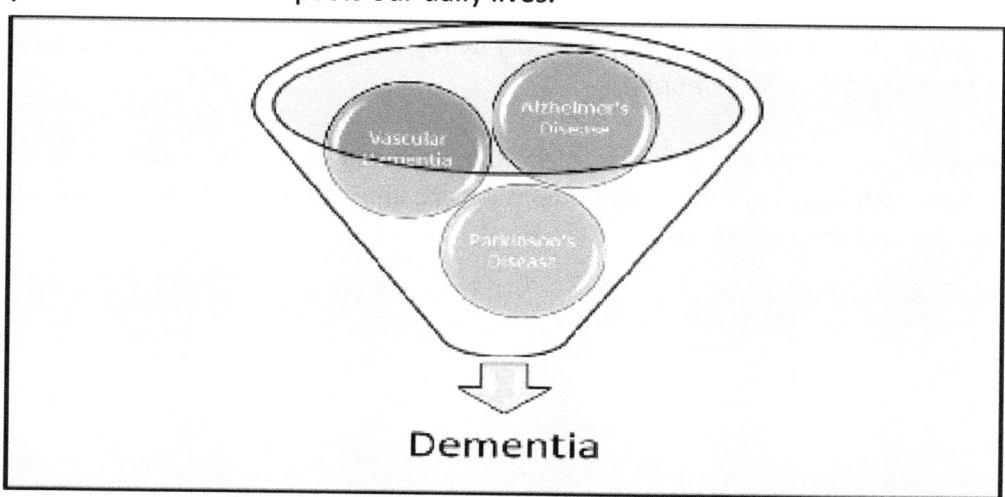

What is Alzheimer's Disease?

Alzheimer's disease is the leading cause of dementia. The most striking symptom is memory loss, especially the loss of recently learned information. Other symptoms include a decline in the ability to learn, reason, make judgments, communicate and carry out daily activities.

As the disease progresses, the person may also experience personality changes, social disengagement and other behaviors, such as anxiety, suspiciousness or agitation. Even though the person may look fine, he or she may begin to have problems with his or her daily routine.

This chart illustrates normal memory loss as we age and examples of memory loss that could be a possible sign of dementia or Alzheimer's:

Normal memory loss as we age	Signs of Alzheimer's
Occasionally making the wrong decision	Frequently showing poor judgment and decision making
Forgetting to pay a bill	Not being able to manage money and household finances
Not remembering what day it is, but remembering later	Not knowing the day, year or season
Trouble remembering the correct word to use sometimes	Not being able to hold a conversation intelligently
Losing car keys or other things every now and then	Losing things and not being able to retrace your steps to find them

Alzheimer's is a growing problem — affecting more than 40% of persons over the age of 65 and increasing numbers of people between the ages of 40-50 years old. According to the Alzheimer's Association more than 5 million Americans are living with Alzheimer's. By the year 2050, this number could rise to 16 million people.

Although there is currently no cure for Alzheimer's, researchers are working to develop new treatments. Research has also shown that effective care and support can improve the quality of life for both patients and their caregivers.

Progression of Alzheimer's

Alzheimer's is a progressive disease that leads to complete disruption of our brain functions and ultimately leads to death. It is important to identify this incurable disease in its early stages. Research suggests that the changes in the brain that lead to Alzheimer's begin many years before symptoms are seen. This includes what physicians and scientists have called 'preclinical' Alzheimer's disease. This can be followed by Mild Cognitive Impairment, when daily living skills remain generally unaffected but the first changes in thinking are seen. Once Alzheimer's disease is diagnosed, there are 3 general stages as follows:

- **Early Stage (Mild Alzheimer's)** – Most persons can drive and live relatively independent, but may start experiencing lapses in their memory and trouble remembering words, locations and things that are familiar to them. Often these changes can lead to withdrawal from social gatherings and may be accompanied by apathy (often mistaken for depression).

- **Middle Stage (Moderate Alzheimer's)** – In this stage, more care is needed for the person suffering as this stage lasts for many years and the decline in memory and thinking gets worse. This is the stage where changes in the person's behavior may begin to show with them experiencing frustration and anger in some cases. The damage in the brain makes it hard for them to express their thoughts and do common tasks like driving and social interactions.

- **Late-Stage (Severe Alzheimer's)** – This is the last stage of the disease and the most difficult stage for both the person diagnosed and for those caring for them. During this stage the person can no longer function, they cannot communicate and eventually lose the ability to control their own body movements. In most people, care is needed around the clock and help doing daily things like bathing and eating.

> *My family and I knew something was going on with my mother because she wasn't acting like she used to. For example, my mother, who usually loves to eat and fix meals, became uninterested in food.*
>
> *I also noticed that she was not as social as she used to be. Instead of hanging out with and talking to adults and being right in the middle of conversation, she would isolate herself from groups or hang out with the children. When we would talk, she would be more guarded in her conversation, almost as if she was carefully watching her words to make sure she said nothing wrong.*
>
> —Anna Mason, Caregiver—

Recognizing the warning signs

Alzheimer's disease advances at different rates for different people. The length of the illness can vary from 3 to 20 years. The areas of the brain that control memory and thinking skills are affected first, but as the disease progresses, cells die in other parts of the brain. Eventually, the person with Alzheimer's may require complete care.

Alzheimer's disease shortens life. People with it are vulnerable to pneumonia, serious falls, infection and other related problems. As the health of a person with Alzheimer's disease begins to fail, Hospice services can be called for necessary support and important end of life care.

To help family and church members recognize the warning signs of Alzheimer's disease, the Alzheimer's Association has developed this...

List of the most common symptoms:

Memory changes that disrupt daily life.

- One of the most common signs of Alzheimer's, especially in the early stages, is forgetting recently learned information. Others include forgetting important dates or events; asking for the same information over and over; relying on memory aids (e.g., reminder notes or electronic devices) or family members for things they used to handle on their own.

What's normal with age? Sometimes forgetting names or appointments, but remembering them later.

Challenges in planning or solving problems.

- Some people may experience changes in their ability to develop and follow a plan or work with numbers. They may have trouble following a familiar recipe or keeping track of monthly bills. They may have difficulty concentrating and take much longer to do things than they did before.

What's normal with age? Making occasional errors when balancing a checkbook.

Difficulty completing familiar tasks at home, at work or at leisure.

- People with Alzheimer's often find it hard to complete daily tasks. Sometimes, they may have trouble driving to a familiar location, managing a budget at work or remembering the rules of a favorite game.

What's normal with age? Occasionally needing help to use the settings on a microwave or to record a television show.

Confusion with time or place.

- People with Alzheimer's can lose track of dates, seasons and the passage of time. They may have trouble understanding something if it is not happening immediately. Sometimes they may forget where they are or how they got there.

What's normal with age? Getting confused about the day of the week but figuring it out later.

Trouble understanding visual images and spatial relationships.
- For some people, having vision problems may be a sign of Alzheimer's. They may have difficulty reading, judging distance and determining color or contrast. In terms of perception, they may pass a mirror and think someone else is in the room. They may not recognize their own reflection.

What's normal with age? Vision changes related to cataracts.

New problems with words in speaking or writing.
- People with Alzheimer's may have trouble following or joining a conversation. They may stop in the middle of a conversation and have no idea how to continue or they may repeat themselves. They may struggle with vocabulary, have problems finding the right word or call things by the wrong name (e.g., calling a "watch" a "hand-clock").

What's normal with age? Sometimes having trouble finding the right word.

Misplacing things and losing the ability to retrace steps.
- A person with Alzheimer's disease may put things in unusual places. They may lose things and be unable to go back over their steps to find them again. Sometimes, they may accuse others of stealing. This may occur more frequently over time.

What's normal with age? Misplacing things from time to time, such as a pair of glasses or the remote control.

Decreased or poor judgment.
- People with Alzheimer's may experience changes in judgment or decision-making. For example, they may use poor judgment when dealing with money, giving large amounts to telemarketers. They may pay less attention to grooming or to keeping themselves clean.

What's normal with age? Making a bad decision once in a while.

Withdrawal from work or social activities.
- A person with Alzheimer's may start to remove themselves from hobbies, social activities, work projects or sports. They may have trouble keeping up with a favorite sports team or remembering how to complete a favorite hobby. They may also avoid social situations because of the changes they have experienced.

What's normal with age? Sometimes feeling weary of work, family and social obligations.

Changes in mood and personality.
- The mood and personalities of people with Alzheimer's can change. They can become confused, suspicious, depressed, fearful or anxious. They may be easily upset at home, at work, with friends or in places where they are out of their comfort zone.

What's normal with age? Developing very specific ways of doing things and becoming irritable when a routine is disrupted.

If you recognize any of these warning signs in yourself or those in your church family, make sure these concerns are brought to the attention of a medical professional. Early diagnosis is an important first step to getting appropriate treatment, care and support.

Diagnosis and Treatment

For persons with dementia, an early diagnosis has many advantages including:

- Relief from anxiety about the unknown problem.
- A better chance to benefit from treatment.
- Time to plan for the future and get legal and financial affairs in order.
- Information to help improve his or her quality of life.

Alzheimer's disease is not the only cause of memory loss or other dementia-like symptoms. Some problems can be reversed if they are caused by treatable conditions like depression, drug interactions, thyroid problems, vitamin deficiencies, or excess use of alcohol. Symptoms caused by Alzheimer's disease cannot be cured, but medications are available which may slow the course of the disease. New treatments are under development.

Families should be encouraged to get a specific diagnosis. Unless the family and doctor know what is causing the symptoms, the choice of an appropriate treatment can be difficult.

Even after the work-up and diagnosis, patients and families may need time to adjust to the news as one patient in Lexington, KY describes:

> "The hardest thing for me to deal with was in the beginning, I didn't believe I had anything. I was putting it all on old age. After I saw what you all represented and I come and had tests and everything, and then I was sent and had a "CAT" scan and you all told me the results and that I had the disease. It has been a problem in a way because when you are thinking one thing and it is something else, it keeps you kind of confused."
>
> *Patient, Polk--Dalton Clinic, Lexington.*
>
> **NOTE:** *The above patient later expressed relief that his problem had a name. His family rallied around him to help.*

Before the diagnosis: Preparing for your Doctor Visit

The possibility of a diagnosis of Alzheimer's can be difficult for both the individual and the family. Prior to seeing your provider the following tips may be helpful in getting yourself prepared:

- Encourage a family member to go with their loved one into the examination room so that they can describe their concerns and hear what the doctor says.
- If the family is uncomfortable speaking about their concerns in front of the patient, have them write out a list of problems and drop it off or fax to the office before the visit.
- Have the family bring all medications, over-the-counter and prescription, to the visit.
- The family should ask the doctor about medications that may help with memory and behavioral problems. New medications are being developed every day.

There is no single test or procedure to determine if someone has Alzheimer's. To get an accurate diagnosis a complete medical evaluation of a person's health and memory status must be done. An initial work-up for Alzheimer's should include the following:

- A complete and accurate medical history. The family should be honest about past or current use of alcohol.
- A neurological and physical exam, which may include brain imaging techniques such as a CT scan, MRI, or PET scan.
- Lab tests (blood and urine) to look for such things as infection or vitamin deficiencies.
- An evaluation of the patient's ability to perform common daily activities, such as balancing a checkbook or taking medications.

- Testing to measure the patient's thinking and memory. These tests may include:
    - General Practitioner Assessment of Cognition (GPCOG) – www.gpcog.com
    - Mini-Cog - Screening for Cognitive Impairment in Older Adults – www.mini-cog.com
    - Montreal Cognitive Assessment Tool (MoCA) – www.mocatest.org
- An interview with the patient's caregivers to hear their story. Some patients are aware of what is happening to them. Be sure to respect their dignity by giving them time to ask questions and express their concerns. The exam can be stressful. The family member can help by taking the person's hand, offering encouragement, and maintaining hope.

Treatment Options

Unfortunately, no cure for Alzheimer's disease has been discovered yet. However, researchers have developed several medications that provide symptomatic benefit during the course of the illness. Medications and other approaches are also available to relieve problems with depression, anxiety, agitation, paranoia, and sleep disturbances. It is important to work with your provider and your family to determine the best treatments and care plan options. In addition to medications, Alzheimer's and its symptoms can also be managed with other cognitive and behavioral therapies that include:

- Counseling and Support Services
- Physical Activity
- Music and Art Therapy
- Social Engagement and Community-based Interventions

Combined with loving care and support, treatment of Alzheimer's is needed to prolong the quality of life for those living with the disease, caregivers and other family members.

The following story describes one caregiver's efforts and summarizes this loving approach:

> "At first it wasn't easy dealing with the personality changes in my uncle. I would get frustrated when I spoke to him because he wouldn't give the right answer to a question I would ask or to things I would say. So I learned to play make believe with him to get things done and make living with him easier. When I would come home from work, I would ask, "Did you go to Louisville today?" and he would say, "Yeah, I went to see my girlfriend." Well, he didn't go anywhere and he doesn't have a girlfriend, but I've learned to have fun with him that way."
>
> —George Ellis, Lexington Caregiver—
>
> **NOTE:** Caregivers who can maintain a sense of humor find that their journey is much easier!

Reducing the Risk of Alzheimer's

As mentioned earlier, there is no cure for Alzheimer's, however there are things that can be done to reduce the risk of developing Alzheimer's and support a healthy brain. The Balm In Gilead refers to these actions as the ...

"Six Pillars of Brain Health."

Regular exercise
   Regular exercise can reduce risk of developing Alzheimer's disease by up to 50%

Healthy diet
   Reduces inflammation that inhibits communication between brain cells

Mental stimulation
   Continuing to learn new things and challenging the brain helps to delay development of Alzheimer's disease

Quality sleep
   Necessary for memory formation and flushing out brain toxins

Stress Management
   Improves key memory area of the brain and promotes nerve cell growth

Active social life
   The better connected we are, the better we fare in our quality of day-to-day life

When peace, like a river, attendeth my way,
When sorrows like sea billows roll;
Whatever my lot, Thou hast taught me to say,
It is well, it is well with my soul.

From "It Is Well With My Soul"
Horatio G. Spafford, 1873

CHAPTER | 2

Dementia and The African American Community

Overview

This chapter describes the impact of Alzheimer's disease on African Americans and provides information on ways faith leaders and members of the community can help address the unique issues and challenges. This chapter will discuss the following:

- **Alzheimer's Disease & African Americans**
- **Role of Pre-existing Health Problems in Alzheimer's Disease Risk**
- **Socioeconomic Challenges for African Americans**

Alzheimer's & African Americans - Sobering Facts

The Alzheimer's Association has identified a growing public health crisis among African Americans calling it "the silent epidemic of Alzheimer's disease." **African Americans are two to three times more likely than whites to develop dementia.** Researchers do not yet understand why this is the case. More than 5 million people in the country have Alzheimer's and this number is expected to double by 2030. It is now estimated that one out of every nine persons over the age of 65 is living with Alzheimer's and one in three will die from this incurable disease.

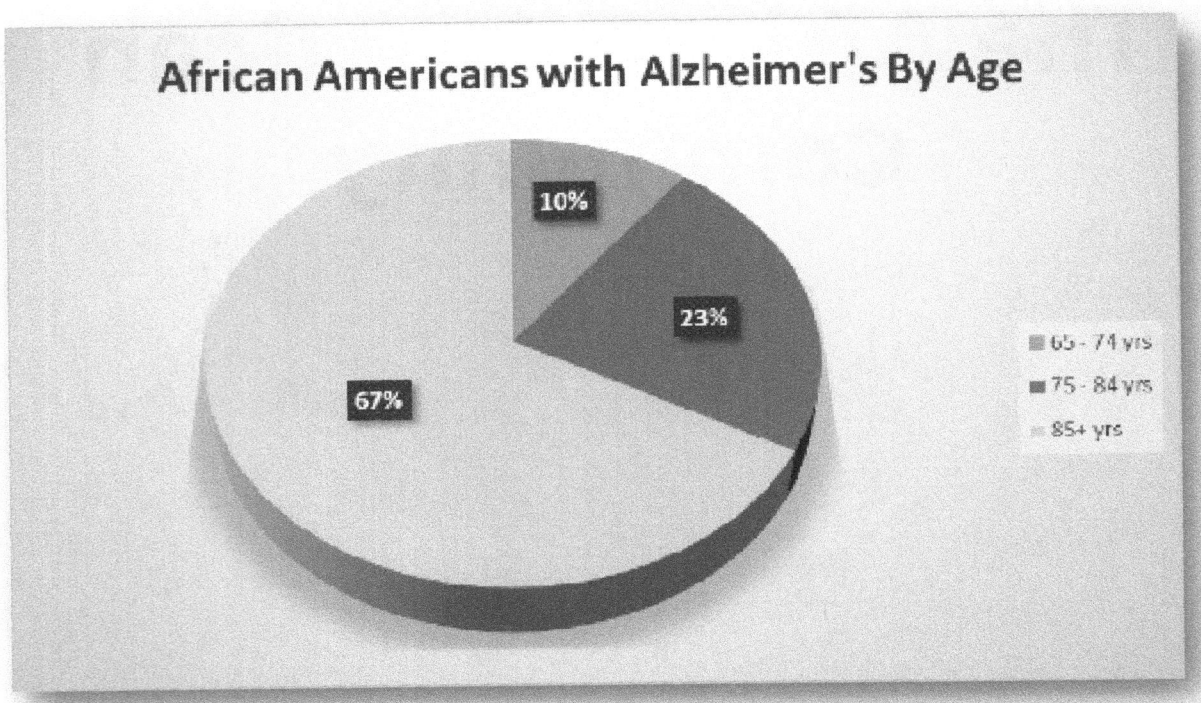

This is particularly sobering as the number of African Americans entering the age of risk (age 65 and over) will more than double from 2.7 million (in 1995) to 6.9 million over the next 23 years. Not only are more and more African Americans developing Alzheimer's but far too many are getting diagnosed in the later stages of disease or not at all. The chart above illustrates the burden of Alzheimer's disease in the Black community.

The rate of Alzheimer's among African Americans between the ages of 65 – 74 years old is four times higher than the rate of whites in the same age range. In 2006, the Health and Retirement Study which surveyed 16,000 participants, aged 55 and older, and captured data on the proportion of Americans aged 55 and older with cognitive impairment by age and ethnicity. The results from the study in the chart above showed that **African Americans were nearly four times as likely to have cognitive impairment at younger ages.**

Women

Disparities in Alzheimer's prevalence can also be seen with its impact among women. More than two-thirds of all persons living with this disease are women. In addition to having the highest rate of Alzheimer's, women also account for two-thirds of those servings as caregivers. This increased burden in women leads to them having nearly double the lifetime risk of developing Alzheimer's.

Heredity

While the greatest known risk factor for Alzheimer's disease is advancing age, other factors may increase one's chance of developing the illness. Another strong risk factor is family history. Those who have a parent, sibling or child with Alzheimer's disease are more likely to develop the disease themselves. The risk increases as the number of family members who have the disease increases. For African Americans, the cumulative risk of dementia among first-degree relatives of a person who has Alzheimer's disease is 43.7%. For spouses of someone with Alzheimer's disease the cumulative risk is 18%. Heredity and environmental factors may both play a role in this cumulative risk.

It is important to note that just because someone in your family has the disease does not mean you will too. Just as if there is no family history of the disease, it does not mean you will not get Alzheimer's disease. A family history of the illness just increases your overall risk.

Role of Pre-existing Health Problems

Data from long-term studies suggest that high cholesterol, high blood pressure, lack of exercise and diabetes may be important risk factors for developing Alzheimer's. The consequences of these discoveries are enormous for African Americans because high blood pressure, high cholesterol and diabetes occur at greater rates among Black people.

Studies suggest that individuals with a history of either high blood pressure or high cholesterol are twice as likely to develop Alzheimer's disease. Those with both risk factors are four times as likely to develop the disease. Sadly, these conditions are common in the African American community. Other health factors that may contribute to the risk of Alzheimer's disease are hypertension and diabetes. Sixty-five (65%) percent of African American Medicare beneficiaries have hypertension, compared to 51% of White beneficiaries.

Risk Factors for Alzheimer's in African Americans

Hypertension	Diabetes
Stroke	Obesity
Lack of physical activity	High cholesterol

These sobering facts suggest that there is an important link between life style and the risk of developing Alzheimer's disease. Many African American churches are introducing health education programs including physical fitness and dieting programs. It seems clear, there are now more reasons than ever for African American churches to embrace these healthy lifestyles.

> *Black folks enjoy certain kinds of foods, fried foods, greasy foods, traditional foods and ethnic foods. Many times these things are very, very harmful to people and they don't know it because it has been such a tradition. These are things that they grew up with, foods they grew up with. Education becomes very important in trying to re-educate people to understand that you need to be concerned about the kinds of foods you eat – fried foods and that kind of thing. And that is not an easy thing, because traveling around as I do, church related, one of the first things that people want to do is feed you!*
>
> *You have to be very selective about what you do in terms of the food that you take in.*
>
> —Bishop Richard Clark, House of God #1, Lexington, Kentucky—

Socioeconomic Challenges for African Americans with Alzheimer's

Alzheimer's disease is one of the costliest chronic diseases. The growing Alzheimer's crisis is helping to bankrupt Medicare. In 2017, total payments for all individuals with Alzheimer's or other dementias are estimated at $259 billion. Medicare and Medicaid are expected to cover $175 billion, or 67 percent, of the total health care and long-term care payments for people with Alzheimer's or other dementias. In addition to these costs, another $56 billion is expected in out-of-pocket expenses related to Alzheimer's and dementia related care. Nearly 1 in every 5 Medicare dollars is spent on people with Alzheimer's and other dementias and by 2050, Alzheimer's is projected to cost more than $1 trillion.

For African Americans the financial cost associated with the care needed for Alzheimer's creates an overwhelming burden on the individuals living with the disease and their family. Other factors that increase the burden for African Americans are summarized in the diagram.

As shown in this graphic, across the spectrum of the disease, socioeconomic factors heavily influence diagnosis, treatment and overall quality of care for African Americans.

This complex dynamic requires a comprehensive and holistic approach to address these challenges.

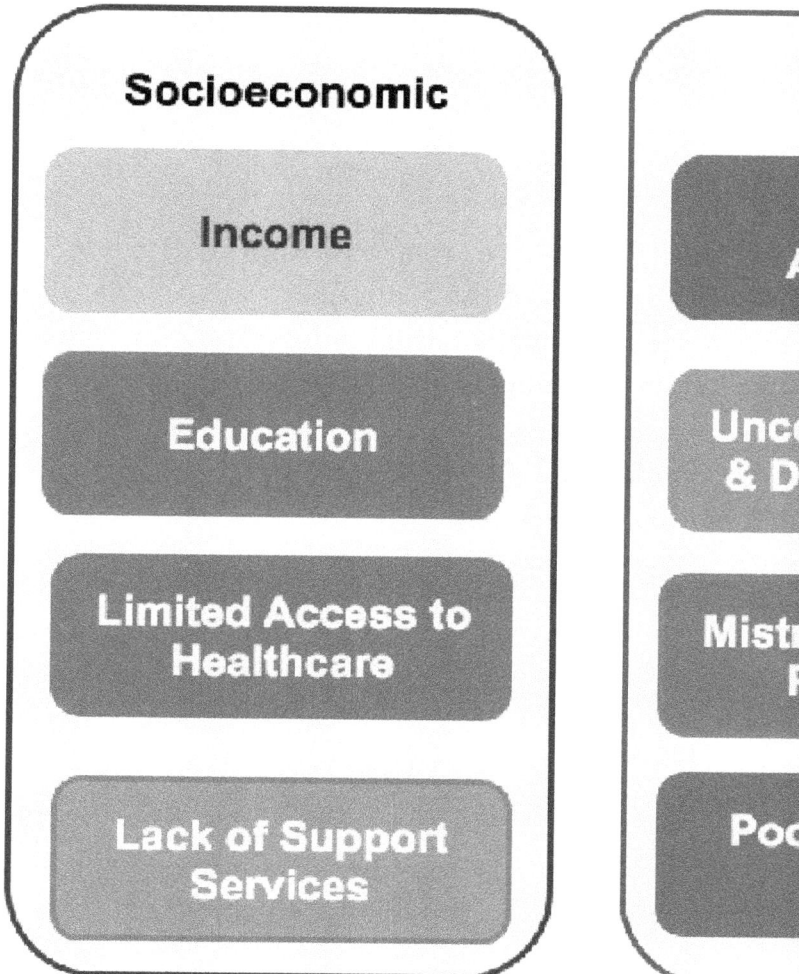
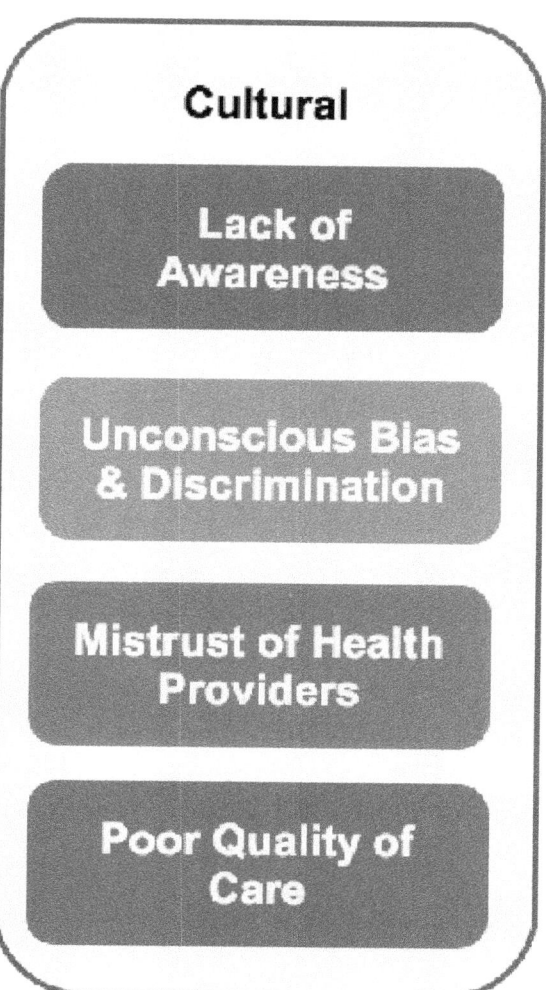

He that dwelleth in the secret place of the most High shall
abide under the shadow of the Almighty.
I will say of the Lord, He is my refuge and my fortress:
my God; in him will I trust.

Psalm 91:1-2

King James Version (KJV)

CHAPTER | 3

Caring for a Person with Dementia

Overview

This chapter will make the case that there is a "right way" and a "wrong way" to help a person with Alzheimer's disease. When caregivers learn some of the tips in this chapter, life will become easier.

The chapter will discuss the following:

- **Understanding the causes of behavior changes associated with dementia**
- **Approaches on responding to behavior changes**
- **Communication challenges and ways to address them**
- **Aggression and other challenging behaviors and ways to address them through activity**
- **Understanding personal care and safety needs for persons with dementia**

Common Causes of Behavior Changes

Coping with challenging or difficult behaviors requires patience, creativity and the ability to live in the moment. There is no magic answer, but there are steps that might help, whether you are offering advice to church members or providing care to a family member in the home.
Persons with dementia have a disease or disorder that is gradually robbing them of the ability to do the things they've always done. This can sometimes cause loneliness, sadness, anger and frustration. On a positive note, it can also cause a person to become happy-go-lucky since he or she may not be aware of his or her losses.

The following sections describe how to create a positive environment for the person and the strategies that a caregiver can employ to reduce challenging behaviors and protect personal dignity. First, keep in mind that the person with dementia will probably not be able to understand reason and logic. The following are some likely causes for behavior changes in the person with dementia.

- Physical discomfort caused by illness, pain or medications.
- Too much noise or activity.
- Not able to recognize familiar places, faces, or things.
- Difficulty completing simple tasks or activities.
- Not able to communicate effectively – to find the right word, answer a question or communicate needs and want.
- Fatigue.
- Depression.
- Constipation.
- Boredom.

It is important to try to identify the cause or causes of the problem behavior and consider possible solutions.

Identify and examine the behavior
- What was the behavior? Was it harmful to the individual or others?
- What happened before the behavior occurred? Did something cause the behavior?

Explore potential solutions
- Is there something the person needs or wants?
- Can you change the surroundings? Is the area noisy or crowded? Is the room well-lighted?
- Are you responding in a calm, supportive way?

Consider different responses in the future
- Did your response help?
- Do you need to explore other potential causes and solutions? If so, what can you do differently?

Responding to Difficult Behaviors
- Stay calm and be understanding.
- Be patient and flexible.
- Don't argue or try to change the person's mind.
- Acknowledge requests and respond to them.
- Don't take behaviors personally.
- Accept the behavior as a reality of the disease and try to work through it.

Approaches to Responding to Behavior Changes

In the last decade, a new phrase has evolved to describe the most effective approach to Alzheimer's care – "person-centered care." The phrase was originally used by British researcher Tom Kitwood and has become the "Golden Rule" for dementia care.

Best Friends' Approach

Virginia Bell, a nationally known social worker and writer from Lexington, Kentucky has said, "Person-centered care suggests that a person with dementia is still just like you and me, with all the same feelings. They want to be heard and valued, loved and cared for. Treat them as you would want to be treated if you had Alzheimer's."

Virginia Bell and her colleague David Troxel have developed a philosophy of care called "Best Friends" that is designed to bring out the best in the person with dementia. This approach to Alzheimer's care reflects the growing belief that much can be done to improve the lives of dementia patients.

The premise of the Best Friends approach is that what a person with Alzheimer's disease really needs is a good friend —a best friend. When the elements of friendship are incorporated into Alzheimer's care, the caregiving relationship becomes less stressful for both the caregiver and the patient. The Best Friends approach maintains that each person with memory loss:

- Is an adult with infinite value apart from loss of memory.
- Has needs of the spirit that must be nurtured with help from others.
- Has feelings about the losses from Alzheimer's disease.
- Has a unique life story.
- Needs something meaningful to "do" and ways to "be."
- Can be helped to experience more positive feelings through quality care.

Life Story Approach

Another approach to handling the changes in behavior for someone with dementia can be referred to as the "Life Story" approach to providing care. As Alzheimer's disease or dementia begins to affect a person's memory, it becomes important that the people involved in his or her care know the person's Life Story. The Life Story involves knowing more than a person's family or occupation. The Life Story is who we are: our hobbies, likes/dislikes, values, roles, faith/spirituality and experiences.

It can be very helpful to create the person's Life Story for future use. Assisting the caregiver in writing the Life Story of their loved one, not only can be an enjoyable process for the caregiver, but also results in a useful tool for the person's care in the future. This written Life Story can be shared with visitors, adult day staff, home care aides, long-term care staff and even physicians to assist in caring for the person. Perhaps you have volunteers in your church who would like to help by compiling someone's life story.

Parts of a "Life Story"

To compose a Life Story, you will need to find out about the person's past. The parts of the Life Story are listed in chronological order for your convenience, but the events are not necessarily only related to those years. For example, someone may have been in military service throughout his or her working life [Bell & Troxel, Best Friends, p. 68].

Childhood
- Birth date
- Birthplace
- Parents, grandparents, brothers and sisters
- Early education
- Pets

Adolescence
- Name of high school
- Favorite classes
- Friends and interests
- Hobbies and sports
- First job

Young Adulthood
- College and work
- Marriage(s)/relationship(s) Family
- Clubs and/or community involvement
- First home
- Military service

Middle Age
- Hobbies
- Work and family roles
- Clubs and organizations, community involvement

Later Years
- Life achievements and accomplishments
- Hobbies Travel Family
- Grandchildren

Other Major Ingredients
   Ethnicity
   Religious background Awards
   Special skills

Collecting the Life Story can be a wonderful project for a Church youth group. The story honors a person's past and can be helpful for the family in the future.

Communication Challenges

A caregiver from Lexington, KY described communication with her Mother, and her approach:

"Well, with my Mom, she is very sensitive about being wrong and things of that nature. So one thing that I try to do is to be sure that I give some credibility to things that she is telling me. I just try to always make sure that I listen to what she is saying."

—Wanda, Caregiver—

The way that Alzheimer's disease affects communication varies from person to person. Early in the disease, people with Alzheimer's disease are often aware of differences in their communication. When aware of their language changes, they may try to cover up. They may make up all or part of a story, become indignant, nervous or anxious. They may use humor to cope with their difficulties or they may admit that they are having a problem. Alzheimer's disease may have the following effects on a person's communication:

- Increasing difficulty expressing ideas and thoughts in words.
- Trouble understanding what has been said.
- Difficulty finding the right words.
- Using familiar words repeatedly.
- Inventing new words to describe familiar objects.
- Difficulty translating thought into action.
- Easily losing train of thought.
- Difficulty organizing words logically.
- Reverting to speaking in a native language.
- Using curse words more often.
- Speaking less often.
- Relying more on nonverbal gestures.

Unfortunately, many people with Alzheimer's disease withdraw from social situations because they don't want others to know about their problems.

> *One caregiver described the change in her sister:*
> *"She didn't want to visit or see her friends anymore. She just did not want to be bothered. And then I would try to get her to play cards and she would say. "I don't want to play cards, what am I going to play cards for?" She loved to play cards. And, of course, it got to the place where she did not want to go to the grocery store. She did not want to go out. Socially she just did not want to be bothered; it was too hard for her."*
>
> —Juanita, Caregiver—

Toolbox 1: Tips on Communication

Effective approach to communicate with your loved one living with Alzheimer's or Dementia

Do not:

- Argue, confront, correct.
- Give orders, make demands.
- Talk down to a person.
- Talk about a person in his or her presence.
- Ask questions that require too many facts.
- Try to explain or prepare too far in advance.
- Take negative comments personally.
- Be insincere by asking questions when you are not offering a choice.
- Give too many choices.
- Take anything for granted.

Do:

- Listen carefully.
- Help the person fill in the blanks.
- Read facial expressions and body language and try to respond appropriately.
- Give compliments.
- Ask opinions.
- Ask open-ended questions.
- Give generous praise.
- Use common sense.
- Enjoy the person.
- Take the blame, apologize.
- Be sincere.
- Use the person's Life Story.
- Use positive language.

[Bell & Troxel, pp. 115-126.]

NOTE: Juanita's sister's withdrawal from society could be caused by her awareness of her losses or by depression. In these situations, caregivers should keep trying creative ideas to keep the person involved in the community. An adult day program can help.

Caregivers may need to develop different ways of communicating with people with dementia. By changing communication strategies, the person may feel more comfortable and in turn, have interactions that are more effective.

Toolbox Tip 2: Communication Challenges & How to Address Them

Repetitive Phrases or Questions

People with Alzheimer's disease sometimes ask the same question or make the same statement over and over. For example, "What time is it? What time is it?" or "I want to go home. . . I want to go home."

For caregivers, this repetition can be maddening!

What does not work is to argue, get angry or try to correct the person.
What can work?

Gently answer the person the first time or help him or her with needed information. Draw the person out by trying to find out what is bothering them:

Person with Alzheimer's	Caregiver Response
"I want to go home"	Mom, tell me about your home.
	Was it in the country or city? Did you enjoy living there?
"What time is it"	What do you need?
	Tell me how you are feeling today.
"Where's Mama?"	Tell me about your mother.
	Was she a good cook like you?
	Was she very strict when you were growing up?

Using this method will often break the repetitive cycle and demonstrate care and concern for the person.

Aggression and Other Behavior Challenges

When a person with Alzheimer's disease is frustrated, scared or unable to communicate, he or she may become aggressive and may even physically strike out. Aggressive behaviors can be caused by many things, including physical discomfort and the inability to understand. If the person is showing signs that he or she may become physically aggressive, review the following list of tips.

Tips for dealing with Aggressive Behaviors:

- **Identify signs of frustration** - Look for early signs of frustration during activities such as bathing, dressing or eating and respond in a calm and reassuring tone.

- **Don't take the behavior personally** - The person isn't necessarily angry with you. He or she may have misunderstood the situation or be frustrated with lost abilities caused by the disease.

- **Don't lecture** - Avoid long explanations and arguments. Be encouraging and don't expect the person to do more than he or she can.

- **Use distractions** - If the person is frustrated because he or she can't unbutton a shirt, distract the person with another activity. Later, you can return to helping the person unbutton the shirt.

- **Communicate directly with the person** - Avoid expressing anger or impatience in your voice or physical action. Instead use positive, accepting expressions, such as "don't worry" or "thank you." Also use touch to reassure and comfort the person.

- **Decrease level of danger** - Assess the level of danger—for yourself and the person with Alzheimer's. You can often avoid harm by simply stepping back and standing away from the person. If the person is headed out of the house and onto the street, more assertive action may be necessary.

- **Avoid using restraint or force** - Unless the situation is serious, avoid physically holding or restraining the person. He or she may become more frustrated and may cause personal harm.

An example of how to handle agitation was provided by one of our caregivers:

> *"Well I've seen, I guess in the last couple of years, I've seen her become more agitated, like if there is a project that she is working on trying to complete. She gets agitated, just like when she loses her train of thought she becomes very agitated...I notice this more so recently, she will get her words mixed up, or if a word doesn't come out exactly correct it bothers her, but I try to make her realize that it doesn't bother me or anyone else. We just help her finish the sentence."*
>
> —Anna, Caregiver—
>
> **NOTE:** *Anna's calm and supportive approach calms her mother.*

Sleep Problems are Common

Sleeping problems experienced by those with Alzheimer's disease and caregiver exhaustion are two of the most common reasons for placement in nursing homes. While experts are not certain how or why sleeping problems occur, many professionals attribute them to late-day confusion or "sundowning." When sleep problems occur, try to plan more active days, restrict sugar and caffeine late in the day and consult your physician.

Wandering

A person with Alzheimer's is likely to wander at some point during the disease. Identifying the cause of the behavior can help reduce its occurrence. One reason wandering is common is that persons get confused about time and place. They head out the door since they think they're late for work or have to get home.

Recommend that church members join the Safe Return program of the Alzheimer's Association for an identity bracelet and other materials. The program has a 24-hour Hotline that can be called to report a wanderer: 800-625-3780.

People with Dementia Benefit from Activities

Life is an activity. Throughout the day, we spend our time working and playing with friends and family or by ourselves. People with Alzheimer's disease often need help to continue to participate in their favorite activities. Participation in activities, including those offered by your faith community, can improve mood and enhance the caregiving relationship.

As one caregiver shared: "I think many of my problems with my husband stem from his boredom — he doesn't have enough to do." This caregiver worked hard to plan more for him to do at church, and enrolled him in an adult day center program. "I didn't think he'd like it but now he looks forward to it."

Purpose of Activities

- To socialize and feel physically close to others.
- To be productive.
- To feel successful.
- To play.
- To build and retain skills.
- To have a sense of control.
- To fill a religious or spiritual need.
- To experience growth and learning.

Some simple activities to do around the home include: folding laundry, drying dishes, setting the table, sweeping the floor, brushing the dog, scrap booking, sorting socks or watering plants.
In the community, examples could include: taking walks, sitting on a park bench and watching the world go by, going to church, attending a short concert or even volunteering to do some simple tasks for a local non-profit group.

Toolbox Tip 3: Activity Planning

Planning Activities

When planning activities and daily tasks to help the person with Alzheimer's disease organize the day, think about:

- What skills and abilities does the person have?
- What does the person enjoy doing?
- Does the person need help beginning activities?
- Does the person have physical problems?

Strategic Approach

- Make the activities part of the daily routine.
- Focus on enjoyment, not achievement.
- Determine what time of day is best for the activity.
- Offer support and supervision.
- Be flexible and patient and stress involvement.
- Help the person remain as independent as possible.
- Simplify instructions.
- Establish a familiar routine.

Environment

- Make activities safe.
- Change your surroundings to encourage involvement.
- Minimize distractions that can frighten or confuse the person.

Personal Care and Safety for Persons with Dementia

People with Alzheimer's disease may need help with routine activities related to grooming and hygiene. This assistance can be a problem because it signifies a loss of independence and privacy. Providing such care is also difficult for caregivers, especially when they assist with activities that interfere with the individual's privacy.

> "When it's time for my mother to bathe or take her medications, she can be resistant to doing these things, and sometimes just be mean. So I've come up with things to say when she doesn't want to do something in particular. If she says something like, "You're not my momma or daddy," I try to put some humor in it and I tell her that I've been reincarnated as them, you have to do it. Or, if she tells my sister the same thing, she'll tell my mother that her mother and father were in her dreams the night before and told my sister to tell my mother to do what she says. Taking this approach makes us all laugh and takes the edge off of difficult moments.
> —Tim, Caregiver—

Bathing

Bathing is often the most difficult personal care activity that caregivers face. Because it is such an intimate experience, the person with Alzheimer's may perceive it as unpleasant, threatening or painful and, in turn, scream, resist and hit.

These behaviors often occur because the person doesn't know what bathing is for or doesn't have the patience to endure the unpleasantness associated with a lack of modesty, being cold or experiencing discomfort. Try the following:

- **Simplify** - Do as much as possible to make the process easier, such as increasing the room temperature and having bath towels nearby.
- **Help the person feel in control** - Involve and coach him or her through each step of the process. You may need to experiment to find out if the person prefers showers or tub baths and what time of day is best.
- **Create a safe and pleasing atmosphere** - Place nonskid adhesives on the floor surface and grab bars in the bathtub to prevent falls. Test water temperatures in advance to prevent burns.

Toileting

People with Alzheimer's disease often experience a loss of bladder and/or bowel control. This loss can be caused by many factors, including medications, stress, a physical condition, the environment or even the person's clothing.

If incontinence is a new problem, consult a doctor to rule out potential causes such as a urinary tract infection, weak pelvic muscles or medications.

Dental Care

Good oral hygiene can be a problem for people with Alzheimer's disease. Brushing is sometimes difficult due to the person's inability to understand and accept assistance from others. In order to help:

- **Provide short, simple instructions** - "Brush your teeth" may be too complex. Instead try: "Hold your tooth brush," "put paste on the brush" and "brush your top teeth."
- **Use a mirroring technique** - Hold a brush and show the person how to brush his or her teeth.
- **Monitor daily oral care** - Brush teeth or dentures after each meal and floss daily. Remove and clean dentures every night and brush the person's gums and the roof of the mouth. If the person refuses to open his or her mouth, try using oral hygiene aids available from your dentist to prop the mouth open. Strained facial expressions during dinner or refusal to eat may indicate oral discomfort.

Caregivers are essential in helping the person maintain oral hygiene, noticing any problems and seeking help from a dentist. Notify the dentist in advance that the person has Alzheimer's disease, so that an oral care routine can be developed.

Safety

A confused person should not be left unattended. However, it is often difficult or impossible to watch the person all of the time. Thus, home-based caregivers need to make their homes as safe as possible. Here are some tips and checklists to address safety concerns.

Kitchen:

- Lock up cleaning supplies.
- Turn off the electricity to the garbage disposal.
- Hide knives and other utensils.
- Put away the toaster, blender and other small appliances.
- Unplug larger appliances such as microwaves.
- Remove the knobs from the stove, or hook up the stove to a hidden gas valve or electric switch.
- Keep a fire extinguisher nearby.
- Clean out the refrigerator regularly.

Bathroom:

- Set the water temperature to 120 degrees.
- Install grab bars in and near the tub and shower.
- Apply textured decals on slippery surfaces.
- Supervise the use of hairdryers, razors and curling irons.
- Remove any locks from the bathroom door.
- Remove any dangerous items from the medicine chest.

Bedroom:

- Avoid using electric blankets.
- Monitor the use of heating pads.
- Install night lights between the bedroom and bathroom.

Garage:

- Put away hand and power tools such as drills, axes, saws and picks.
- Limit access to large equipment such as lawnmowers, weed-wackers and snow-blowers.
- Lock up poisonous products such as fertilizers and flammable liquids (gas & oil).

Throughout the House:

- Disguise outdoor locks or install deadbolts.
- Remove or tape down throw rugs and carpeting to reduce the risk of falls.
- Apply colored decals to large windows and sliding glass doors.
- Remove poisonous plants.
- Create an even level of lighting near doorways and stairways and between rooms.
- Remove objects that block walking paths.

Outside:
- Disconnect gas grills.
- Lock gates to fences.
- Supervise the person in areas that are not enclosed.

Other tips:
- Remove guns from the home.
- Consider some kind of confusion lock or buzzer to alert you if the person leaves the home unattended.

A good resource is Mark and Ellen Warner's book: ***The Complete Guide to Alzheimer's Proofing Your Home***: Purdue Univ. Press, 2000.

Driving

Safe driving habits require quick reactions, alert senses and split-second decision making. For a person with Alzheimer's disease, driving inevitably becomes difficult.

For most of us, the restriction of driving privileges means a loss of independence. People with dementia may refuse to give up their car keys because they have similar feelings and do not want to depend on others for transportation. They also may not have the insight and judgment to realize that they should not drive.

A diagnosis of Alzheimer's disease does not necessarily mean that a person has lost the ability to drive. Caregivers should evaluate the person regularly to determine if it is safe for him or her to continue driving.

Tips on stopping the person with Alzheimer's disease from driving:
- Ask a doctor to write a "do not drive" prescription.
- Control access to the car keys.
- Disable the car by removing the distributor cap or battery.
- Park the car on another block or in a neighbor's driveway.
- Arrange for alternate transportation.

Be sensitive and supportive during this no-driving period, as the person may feel angry and depressed. A winning strategy can be to turn the matter over to the Department of Motor Vehicles. A member of the public or the person's doctor can report the person to DMV who will be an independent decision maker about an individual's ability to drive safely.

I will lift up mine eyes unto the hills, from whence cometh my help.
My help cometh from the Lord, which made heaven and earth.
He will not suffer thy foot to be moved: he that keepeth thee
will not slumber.
Behold, he that keepeth Israel shall neither slumber nor sleep.
The Lord is thy keeper: the Lord is thy shade upon thy right hand.
The sun shall not smite thee by day, nor the moon by night.
The Lord shall preserve thee from all evil: he shall preserve thy soul.
The Lord shall preserve thy going out and thy coming in from
this time forth, and even for evermore.

Psalm 121

King James Version (KJV)

CHAPTER | 4

A Caregiver's Journey – Taking Care of You Too

Overview

Alzheimer's is slow and progressive, and caregivers often have a difficult journey. In many ways, they too are "patients." The following chapter offers ways to help family caregivers in your church and the community. This chapter discusses the following:

- **Challenges of being a Caregiver**
- **Stress and the Caregiver**
- **Supporting Caregivers to plan for what's ahead**

Challenges of being a Caregiver

Caring for someone with Alzheimer's disease can take a toll on the caregiver's physical, emotional and financial health. As the disease progresses, caregivers need to devote more attention to their loved ones. At the same time, they should not forget their own needs. The most important needs caregivers say that they have are:

- Information about caregiving.
- Social support from friends and family.
- A break from caregiving responsibilities.
- Help in planning for the future.

Caregiving refers to attending to another individual's health needs. It often includes assistance with one or more activities of daily living, such as bathing and dressing, as well as multiple instrumental activities of daily living, such as paying bills, shopping and transportation. Nationally, approximately 83% of help provided to older adults in U.S. comes from family members, friends or other unpaid caregivers. In 2016, caregivers of people with Alzheimer's and other dementias provided an estimated 18.2 billion hours of informal or unpaid assistance to their family members and loved ones.

African Americans are more likely to take care of their family members in the home without the use of outside help. These caregivers can benefit from education and increased awareness of the disease. They also need special encouragement to overcome disease stigma and to utilize services early and often. Caregiving demands may be perceived differently depending on who is providing the primary care, as a patient describes:

> *"My wife has been more affected by the disease than our children have. The children they have the wrong concept about it. Every time they are here, they are like – how are you feeling? Dad, can I do this? They are going to make me an invalid."*
>
> *—Caregiver—*
>
> **NOTE:** *A family meeting facilitated by a trusted party, perhaps a clergy member, can help families clarify roles and successfully travel the caregiving journey.*

Stress and The Caregiver

More than 80 percent of people who care for Alzheimer's patients report that they frequently experience high levels of stress, and nearly half say they suffer from depression. Many caregivers don't recognize their needs, fail to do anything about them, or simply don't know where to turn for help.

Too much stress can be damaging to both caregivers and the people for whom they provide care. Recognizing the signs and learning how to reduce stress can help.

Below is a family member's description of how she dealt with her stress:

> *"Sometimes I get tired and I think, "Oh, I cannot do this anymore". I go see my Mom every day, but usually if I take a few minutes to reflect and pray and so forth, I feel better about it. It kind of seems like well maybe this is what I'm supposed to be doing. Maybe this is what God has chosen me to do, to help a person who really needs my help.*
>
> *—Wanda, Caregiver—*
>
> *NOTE: Wanda's faith has given her comfort and purpose.*

Warning Signs of Caregiver Stress:

- Denial
- Anger
- Social withdrawal
- Anxiety
- Depression
- Exhaustion
- Sleeplessness
- Irritability
- Lack of concentration
- Health problems

Suggestions for reducing stress:

- Identify and use community resources.
- Become educated about Alzheimer's disease and caregiving techniques.
- Ask for help from family, friends, and the community.
- Watch your diet, exercise, and get plenty of rest.
- Talk with your physician and learn to use relaxation techniques.
- Accept changes as they occur.
- Plan for the future – legal and financial.
- Be realistic about what you can do.
- Don't feel guilty if you lose your patience or can't do everything.

Grief & Loss

Family caregivers can expect to experience feelings of loss, especially as their lives and the people they love are changed by disease. The natural phases of grieving usually involve denial, anger, guilt, physical symptoms and eventually acceptance. However, it is important to know that everyone grieves differently.

To cope with the grieving process, those providing care should consider the following:

- Confront their feelings.
- Accept guilt as a common part of loss and grief.
- Find ways to forgive themselves and others.
- Share their feelings with a friend, support group, therapist or spiritual leader.
- Learn to feel comfortable accepting and celebrating good things in their life.

Supporting Caregivers to Plan Ahead

Legal and Financial Issues

Alzheimer's disease brings with it important legal concerns. Individuals diagnosed with Alzheimer's and their families should plan for the future. Legal planning should begin soon after a diagnosis is made and should include documents that authorize another person to make health care and financial decisions and identifies appropriate plans for long-term care.
If the person with Alzheimer's disease has legal capacity —the level of thinking necessary to sign official documents— he or she should be a part of the legal planning process.

Legal documents that should be considered in legal planning for individuals with dementia include:

- **Durable Power of Attorney**

A durable power of attorney document gives the person with Alzheimer's disease the opportunity to authorize another person, usually a trusted family member or friend, to make decisions when he or she is no longer competent.

- **Power of Attorney for Health Care or Health Care Surrogate**

These documents appoint someone the person trusts to make all decisions about health care, including choices about health care providers, medical treatment and facilities. For people in the later stages of Alzheimer's, the health care surrogate will choose care services and make end-of-life decisions.

- **Living Will**

In a living will, the person with Alzheimer's disease expresses his or her decision on the use of artificial life support systems.

Finding An Attorney

It can be important to find an attorney who is familiar with "Elder Law." Elder Law covers those legal issues that affect older people. In the past, attorneys serving the legal needs of the elderly tended to focus on estate planning. They dealt with the financial needs of the healthy retiree and focused on the distribution of estates at death.

As America's older population has grown, the field of Elder Law also has grown. Elder Law encompasses aspects of planning for aging, illness and incapacity, including:

- Disability Benefit Applications and Appeals.
- Estate Planning.
- Guardianship/Conservatorship.
- Long Term Care Planning.
- Medicaid and Planning.
- Powers of Attorney/Advanced Directives.
- Social Security and Retirement Benefits.

There are a number of additional fields which apply to Elder Law. However, most Elder Law attorneys do not specialize in every field. It is important to hire an attorney who understands those matters of greatest concern to the patient and caregiver. It is also important to consider the attorney's level of experience and the amount of time devoted to Elder Law issues.

If one's affairs are simple, internet resources and self-help legal offices may save the family money. Many local senior centers or area agencies on aging offer low-cost or free legal services.

Words of Wisdom for Caregivers

"No man (or woman) is an Island"

Many caregivers make the mistake of isolating themselves and waiting until they are exhausted to take advantage of available community services.

A faith community should encourage members to be open about aging issues and elder care. Caregivers may benefit from support groups and adult day care for their family members. Day centers get the person out of the house for supervised activity. Many day centers are low cost or have fees based on a sliding scale, so caregivers should be encouraged to try these programs without being discouraged by potential costs.

Another way churches can help is by writing about caregiving issues in the church bulletin or newsletter. Personal testimonials make those suffering aware that they are not alone. If a son or daughter, husband or wife, writes about their caregiving experiences and their needs, it may encourage others to come forward and ask for help.

Words of Wisdom from a Caregiver

One hero in the African American community who took her despair and turned it into a positive mission to help others is Lela Knox Shanks. She found herself traveling the caregiving journey when her husband was diagnosed with Alzheimer's disease.

Among the lessons she learned were:
- Attitude determines outcome.
- Refuse to be a victim.
- The Alzheimer's Disease experience is part of a "Grand Design."
- Tap into your inner strengths.
- Creativity is infinite.
- Connect faith to your daily life.

She cared for her husband Hughes until his death in 2000 and wrote a best-selling book, "Your Name Is Hughes Hannibal Shanks: A Caregiver's Guide to Alzheimer's," about her experiences. Her final recommendation to caregivers, like herself, is: "acceptance takes away the burden," and "in the end, only love matters."

CHAPTER | 5

Keeping the Faith: Churches Response to Alzheimer's

Overview

Alzheimer's disease and other dementias are physically, emotionally, and spiritually challenging for both those living a diagnosis and their loved ones. Our spirituality and faith are important characteristics of not only who we are but also connect us to something greater than ourselves. This chapter will discuss how churches can support persons living with Alzheimer's and their caregivers in their journey to "keep the faith" by considering the following:

- Understanding Importance of Religion and Faith in Persons with Alzheimer's
- Giving Spiritual Care
- The Power of Prayer
- Church and Caregiver Support
- Supporting Youth
- Do you have a Sister Jones?

Importance of Religion and Faith

In support groups, caregivers often ask: "What happens to my mother's faith if she forgets it? Does that mean she has lost her relationship to God?" Most religious leaders and experts on Alzheimer's disease would answer "No." Alzheimer's disease may take away the person's ability to think and reason, but the spirit of the person remains and is shown in other ways, including their experience of the present moment. Some experts have suggested that Alzheimer's disease may put the person in a more spiritual space, as they are no longer distracted by TV news, cell phones, news of the day, or problems of the world.

Research has found that those patients with Alzheimer's disease with higher levels of religiosity and spirituality had a slower progression of the disease as shown by their scores on tests of memory and thinking (Kaufman, Freedman & Koenig, 2005). Such research suggests that families should support the patient's remaining abilities and help them to keep religion in their lives.

Families may need to be reminded that God is not angry with them and is not punishing their family, and that He has not forgotten them. They should be encouraged to keep God as a part of their family and help their family member in the expression of faith and hope.

Some suggestions for keeping the person with dementia connected to his or her faith include:

- Singing and listening to familiar hymns and other religious music
- Reading from the Bible or other sacred texts
- Praying or participating in prayers given by others
- Sharing in religious rituals such as the cross, or saying the rosary
- Seeing and feeling the love of God in the actions of their caregivers and others who love them

(Bell & Troxel, A Dignified Life, p. 212)

One family member described her Mom's faith as follows:

> "I noticed that Mom's faith was still very high even though there might be things that she has forgotten. She taught Sunday school for 32 years and she is always talking to people wherever we go about the Lord."
>
> —Ms. Marie Allen—
>
> **NOTE:** *Faith is one way patients can feel connected with others and maintain their dignity.*

Giving Spiritual Care

Caregivers should understand that nurturing the spiritual being is not limited to church activities. God's presence in nature can be shared through walks or drives in the country with the patient.

Spiritual life can be enhanced through:
1. Participating in the arts including music, painting, or poetry.
2. Being outside on a beautiful spring day.
3. Enjoying a rainbow.
4. Walking along a river, lake or ocean to experience the majesty of nature.

Virginia Bell, author of "A Dignified Life: The Best Friends Approach to Alzheimer's Care, A Guide for Family Caregivers", has written that while many people have a religious background and are members of a faith community, all of us have a spirit.

A church community can nurture both!

The Power of Prayer

A continued fellowship with God may be essential for maintaining dignity and quality of life for the person with dementia. For the person for whom religion and prayer have been an important part of life, efforts should be made to allow the continued practice of faith in a manner as similar as possible to what brought comfort to the person before the illness.

Attendance at church services may become difficult as the disease progresses and crowds become a distraction that interferes with communion with God.

Individuals with dementia move through the disease at different speeds and with different symptoms. They may suffer from losses that affect vision and hearing as well as the ability to think and understand the written word. Early in the disease attendance at church services and other religious events may provide a welcome sense of being normal. As the disease progresses, attendance at shorter services or Bible studies may be an option as the length of a regular service may be too tiring for the person and large groups of people may be upsetting. Visits to the sanctuary, when there is no service, may also allow the person with dementia to continue to connect with their earlier religious experiences.

For those persons, who cannot put words together to form a prayer and whose mind may not recall how to pray, praying with them, reciting old prayers, or singing hymns may help the person to recapture the peace that praying brought earlier in life. Long elaborate prayers are unlikely to provide comfort and may even create anxiety when the words or meaning are not understood. Identifying the person's favorite Bible verses and observing the person's reactions when different scripture and prayers are read will help to determine the words and situations that create the most positive spiritual experience. Try to determine whether a particular physical time, location, or position makes the person feel closer to God. If at home, the person may have had a special chair or place in which he or she prayed or may have always prayed at a particular time of day. A simple prayer before meals said with the person is usually easy to include in the day's activities and may provide important continuity to the person's spiritual existence. When assisting with prayer, it may be helpful to remind the person to close his or her eyes, bow the head, or kneel if that was a part of how they prayed before the disease. These rituals are also helpful for blocking out distractions during the time for prayer and may allow the person to recapture the experience of prayer.

It is important to remember that persons with dementia continue to experience emotion, and their moods may change from day to day. Just as with anyone else, a prayer may be appropriate one day but not appropriate the next. However, prayers of praise to God as well as prayers of hope and gratitude for life are likely to be spiritually uplifting.

The Lord's Prayer is not only familiar, but is an excellent example of praising God in the humility of our humanity and asking God's forgiveness, guidance, and protection.

Examples of Other Prayers:

Simple Prayer Before Meals:
> Bless us, O Lord! And these Thy gifts, which we are about to receive from Thy bounty, through Christ our Lord. Amen.

Simple Prayer After Meals:
> We give Thee thanks for all Thy benefits, O Almighty God, who lives and reigns the world without end. Amen.

> May the souls of the faithful departed, through the mercy of God, rest in peace. Amen.

NOTE: Saying familiar prayers or being part of a ritual is comforting to many persons with dementia.

Churches and Caregiver Support

Churches play a major role in American society, particularly in the African American community. In general, congregations are getting older, described as the "graying of the congregation," thus churches will be facing more and more issues related to caring for increased numbers of older members in the near future. (Pieper and Garrison, 1992).

Caregivers tend to continue their participation in religious communities, while decreasing participation in most other activities (George and Gwyther, 1986). This finding provides church leaders with an important message: families are turning to the church in their greatest time of need – even while giving up other activities. Sensitive church leaders will return this confidence with support and concern. The church is a place for community support for African Americans of all ages (Taylor and Chatters, 1993). Again, church leaders and volunteers play an essential role in helping families and individuals dealing with Alzheimer's.

Eleven Ways Churches Can Help

1. Be informed! Host educational events about aging, Alzheimer's disease and caregiving and remember that education is an on-going process. Information and resources change over time. Stay connected with your Center on Aging and local Alzheimer's Association.
2. Host a support group for family caregivers, or inform your members where groups are being held. Provide a listing of support groups and other dementia activities in your church bulletin.
3. Encourage your church volunteers and leaders to learn about Alzheimer's disease and dementia and to be a resource for families in need.
4. Offer alternative shorter services or home-visits for persons who find larger crowds upsetting. Try to prevent patient and caregiver isolation.
5. Develop a Church Respite program, where friendly visitors help out in the home or provide companionship a few hours a week. Don't forget those church members in nursing homes.
6. If needed, develop an adult day program perhaps in cooperation with other churches or community groups.
7. Invite early-stage persons to continue to volunteer for tasks that may bring them satisfaction such as folding a church newsletter or light housekeeping/gardening.
8. Build a relationship with the Sanders-Brown Center on Aging at the University of Kentucky and the local Alzheimer's Association.
9. Encourage retired nurses to develop a church wellness program.
10. Encourage congregation members to adopt a healthier lifestyle to reduce the risk of Alzheimer's disease.
11. Download resources from The Balm In Gilead and participate in Memory Sunday.

Engaging Youth

Youth and young people whose loved ones are dealing with Alzheimer's disease and dementia also need support. Creating a program and environment that provides education and support to youth is another way for churches to address Alzheimer's in their congregation and community. Faith leaders and youth ministers can create a faith-based youth program that includes awareness and education about healthy aging and Alzheimer's disease. This is important to support youth who may have concerns about a grandparent or loved one.

Tips to consider when creating a youth program focusing on dementia and Alzheimer's include:

- Their enthusiasm and interest can get a whole congregation involved.
- Encourage church youth to sponsor educational programs, volunteer to make visits to church members at home or in assisted living/nursing home settings, or to volunteer at a day center.
- Channel enthusiasm for a project at school into broader community service. Keep young people educated and involved with issues that affect their family and community.

Do you have a Sister Jones in your Congregation?

Sister Jones is an 84-year old woman. She and her husband were active members of St. Matthew's Church for over forty years. Brother Jones was diagnosed with Alzheimer's disease five years ago. Since then, his wife has been the primary caregiver and they have not been as involved in their church community. Sister Jones attends services almost every week, but does not participate in volunteer projects as much as she used to. Sometimes her husband accompanies her to church but he just sits—smiling and looking around. Sister Jones' health is declining and she told her pastor that she feels ill and tired.

Sister Jones has not used formal services such as adult day care or home-delivered meals because she does not think she can afford them and she is not involved in a support group because she cannot leave Brother Jones alone. She would greatly benefit from informal support.

If a few church members would alternate providing respite a few hours per week, Sister Jones could attend church activities or meetings of others caring for a person with Alzheimer's disease (fellowship group) and she would have the needed break she requires, knowing that her husband is safe. Members of the congregation could deliver meals to the couple a few times per week, relieving Sister Jones of the responsibility of preparing dinner, and giving her a break. These simple tasks require only a minor commitment on the part of the congregation, yet would have a positive impact on Sister Jones' sense of well-being. Do you have a Sister Jones in your congregation? What do you have in place to help her?

CHAPTER | 6

Importance of Participating in Research and Clinical Studies

Overview

Research is a systematic or organized way doctors, researchers, and other healthcare professionals work to identify new or improved ways to treat, manage, and even cure diseases. This chapter will discuss why it is important for African Americans to participate in research studies and share some insight from research efforts in Alzheimer's targeting African Americans.

Importance of Participation in Research

Many people dealing with Alzheimer's disease want to do something to help find a better treatment or a cure. They want to help others. One way to help is to participate in research. Not only does research help future generations, but it may help those participating in the study as well. Study participants may receive new medications or free check-ups as a part of their participation.

Due to a mistrust of the healthcare system, historical barriers, and a lack of awareness of research opportunities, African Americans have not been well represented in research studies. This lack of representation has meant that knowledge related to how Alzheimer's disease affects African Americans differently than whites is lacking. Participation in research is necessary to improve drug therapies, patient care and enhance knowledge related to Alzheimer's disease and other forms of dementia.

African Americans should be reassured that safeguards to ensure the protection of all participants in research are now in place to prevent earlier abuses from occurring again.

For example, all researchers must now obtain Institutional Review Board approval before they can ask anyone to be a part of their research. This approval requires that potential risks and benefits along with specific study requirements be clearly explained to all participants. Participants give their voluntary consent to participate and know that they can withdraw at any time. These protections benefit all research participants.

If individuals with dementia or their families are interested in participating in research, they will want to seek answers to the following kinds of questions.

1. Is there any risk to the person with dementia? If so, how much?
2. Does the potential benefit outweigh the risk to the patient or the family? For example, if a new drug could help mother now, and the only potential side effect is a stomachache, the family may decide that the risk is acceptable.
3. Does the family know the group doing the research? Are they respected in the community? Do they ask, not require, participation and explain exactly what will be involved including how much time is required?
4. Are the researchers' explanations provided in language that is easy to understand?
5. Will researchers report their findings to you?
6. Is the program free of charge?
7. Will out-of-pocket expenses (like transportation) be reimbursed?

A Participant's Perspective

The following interview describes the attitude and feelings of a research participant.

This dialogue captures many of the important issues involved in research participation.

When I say the word research, what does that mean to you?

"Research gives an opportunity to learn more about diseases such as Alzheimer's disease. When research findings are published it enables us to learn more, and it makes me proud to be a research volunteer. My eyes have been opened to the necessity of knowing more about the devastation that can happen to the human brain and ways that we can prevent or at least delay that devastation. Continued research gives me hope for a cure."

Some people have mixed feelings towards research participation as they fear it may be harmful to them. How do you feel about that statement?

> I know about the research at Tuskegee, but I also know that there are safeguards in place that prevent that from happening again. The information I have received from research has been extremely helpful, and I continue to read and learn. I think research is beneficial because without research what little knowledge we have about diseases that exist in our world today, these diseases would continue to be unknown factors in human lives. Research provides more information and more possibilities for treatments and solutions to eliminate these diseases.

What would you say motivates you to participate in research and is trust in the researchers a big factor?

> "I suppose it is my belief that my participation could be positive enough to help somebody else as well as myself. Trust is not as important because something as serious as this disease should not be limited or curtailed by my personal mistrust alone. My skepticism might cause me to be vigilant, but when I balance, my personal discomfort against the help that could be provided, I want to be a part of the help that is provided. It takes everyone, and I must do my part.
>
> Through faith in God and my years of ministry, I have learned that it takes patience and understanding to forget about self and do what you can to help others. My work as a research participant affords me the opportunity to exercise the power of that faith to continue in the battle to eradicate Alzheimer's disease for all humankind. We know more about this disease than ever before, and I don't believe God brought us this far to leave us.
>
> —Rev. Reynolds, Research Participant—

Some African Americans don't want to be involved in research. Why do you think that is?

> African Americans are often a suspicious people, and that is understandable- given the history of discrimination in our country. Today things are better, but racial discrimination still exists and is often more subtle. Because the possibility of unfair treatment always looms, we need reassurance and definite proof that researchers are treating us fairly and are working to produce positive results that will benefit not just the majority but African Americans as well.

Do you think it is important for African Americans to participate in research?

> I KNOW it is important! If positive progress is to be made, we need to know how this disease affects all races and genders. Alzheimer's disease can be far too devastating to limit studies to one race or one gender and to make assumptions about the others. Our studies must be thorough and inclusive so that we will know what it takes to find appropriate medications and an eventual cure that will benefit everyone.

Have you told other people that you're involved in research?

> Yes, I use every chance I get to tell others about research and its importance. I believe that those who are recruiting, treating patients, and doing the research need encouragement, cooperation, respect, guidance, and the love of Almighty God as well as the support of research participants. Those of us who are already involved in research participation can be ambassadors for the cause. Even though it must always be a personal choice to participate, sometimes we can lead by example.

Clinical Trials: What Are They?

Clinical trials look at new drugs or vaccines that may help treat or prevent disease, look at ways of detecting or finding out more about a disease, and monitor new drugs or evaluate new combinations of established treatments. The main goal of clinical trials is to see if these new drugs or technologies are safe and work to cure or treat the illness being studied.

Why should minorities participate?

In the past, most drugs were tested on white men. Groups such as African Americans, Hispanic Americans, Native Indians, Asian Americans, and women, were usually not a part of drug clinical trials. Studies have shown that drugs work differently among various people. It is important to make sure we understand how to use drugs to get the best results in all people.

Phases of Clinical Trials

A new drug must travel a long path before it becomes available to consumers.

Phase I: To enter phase I, a new drug must go through extensive laboratory testing which shows that it is safe for human consumption and use. Once proven safe, researchers are then able to observe the drug's effects on the human population. During Phase I, researchers study how the drug interacts with our bodies and what potential side effects it may have. About 70% of drugs move on to Phase II.

Phase II: The drugs that reach phase II are then studied for their treatment efficacy (how well they work to fight the disease). One group of research participants will get the study drug and another group often gets a placebo pill; this is a pill that closely resembles the study drug but is not active medication (it is often a sugar pill). The group getting the placebo pill serves as a comparison group when treatment results are evaluated to fully understand the effects of the new drug on the person with the disease. Today, given existing medicines for Alzheimer's disease, people who are taking these medicines can also participate in studies of potentially new treatments. About 1 in 3 drugs will continue to Phase III.

Phase III: Phase III is similar to Phase II but expands the study to include many more research participants. This provides a more thorough understanding of the drug's effects in the general population and determines if it is a safe and appropriate treatment for a certain disease. About 70% to 90% of drugs will pass Phase III and continue to the final phase of testing, Phase IV. At the conclusion of Phase III, most drugs can be put on the national market for use.

Phase IV: After drugs are put on the market, pharmaceutical companies complete post marketing trials and keep track of side effects. The new drug is compared to similar drugs on the market to see if it is more beneficial or if it has fewer side effects. These drugs are also monitored for long-term effectiveness and impact on the individual's quality of life. Cost effectiveness is also evaluated. At the conclusion of this phase, depending on the results, the drug will remain on the shelves or be taken off.

Benefits of Participating in Clinical Trials

- Opportunity to possibly get a new treatment before it's available to the general population.
- Possibility of being among the first to benefit from a new treatment or new information about a current treatment.
- Special care and close oversight by trial doctors.
- Possibility of free health screenings and exams.
- Opportunity to contribute to medical and scientific knowledge, possibly for your good and/or the good of future generations.
- For some clinical trials, participants are paid for travel to the research site and to undergo certain medical procedures.

Lessons from the African American Dementia Outreach Partnership (AADOP):

Based on the experience of staff and faculty of AADOP, individuals working with African American families coping with Alzheimer's disease should consider the following:

Old wounds can be slow to heal. Many African Americans remember times in the past when doors in the healthcare community were closed to them. Churches will need to help their families identify trusted health care providers including well trained physicians who can assist in the dementia diagnosis. Don't forget to check with the Alzheimer's Association for physician listings.

Family is important - African American families often include multi-generational households, and respect for elders is strong. Family meetings can be a good idea, but remember that there are often multiple decision makers in a family.

Identify decision makers, and work to educate them about Alzheimer's disease and the decisions that they will need to make.

Faith is a part of daily life – African Americans continue to be active in faith communities. Churches can play an essential role in identifying people struggling with symptoms of dementia and encouraging the use of services. Also, caregivers often need the kind of informal support that can be best provided by religious congregations. Such support, if adequate and timely, has the potential to reduce stress and related health problems for the caregiver. Encourage your church elders to develop a proactive approach to helping members travel their journey with dementia. Be a source of strength!

Remember to stay personal - Tell stories - Many caregivers are willing to share stories about their experiences. Encourage person-to-person exchange; it's the best way to share information and possible solutions to specific problems.

Offer church based services - If support groups that are offered through your Alzheimer's Association are not well attended by your church members, the church may need to sponsor a group with help from the Alzheimer's Association.

Address the stigma of Alzheimer's - Many in the African-American community have untrue ideas about Alzheimer's disease and dementia. Recognition that Alzheimer's disease is a medical problem requires education. One way AADOP has encouraged the use of services is to offer free memory check-ups. These screenings stress the importance of "enhancing brain power." Many in the African-American community have responded in a positive way to this approach and have then shared concerns about older family members. Check to see if free memory check-ups are available through trained professionals in your community and consider offering the service through the church just as you do with blood pressure screenings. Also, families who may be unable to deal directly with dementia will usually respond to an emphasis on the importance of keeping their loved one safe in the home.

Keep it social - Even when talking about the serious topic of caring for a family member with Alzheimer's disease, the best meetings usually include social time with coffee and refreshments or other ways to "break bread." Meetings with food allow people to talk informally and create a comfortable, non-judgmental setting to discuss changes in memory.

REFERENCES

African American Network Against Alzheimer's. (2013). Fact Sheets. Retrieved from African American Network Against Alzheimer's: http://www.usagainstalzheimers.org/networks/african-americans/fact-sheets

African American Network Against Alzheimer's. (2013, September). The Cost of Alzheimer's and other Dementias on African Americans. Retrieved from Us Against Alzheimer's African Americans Against Alzheimer's Network: http://www.usagainstalzheimers.org/networks/african-americans

Alzheimer's Association. (2002). African Americans and Alzheimer's Disease: The Silent Epidemic. Retrieved from Alzheimer's Association: https://www.alz.org/national/documents/report_africanamericanssilentepidemic.pdf

Alzheimer's Association. (2009). 10 Early Signs and Symptoms of Alzheimer's. Retrieved from Alzheimer's Association: http://www.alz.org/national/documents/checklist_10signs.pdf

Alzheimer's Association. (2016, October). What is Alzheimer's? Retrieved from Alzheimer's Association: http://www.alz.org/national/documents/brochure_basicsofalz_low.pdf

Alzheimer's Association. (2017). 2017 Alzheimer's Disease Facts & Figures. Retrieved from Alzheimer's Association: http://www.alz.org/documents_custom/2017-facts-and-figures.pdf

Alzheimer's Association. (n.d.). Stages of Alzheimer's. Retrieved from Alzheimer's Association: http://www.alz.org/alzheimers_disease_stages_of_alzheimers.asp

Centers for Disease Control and Prevention. (2007). The Healthy Brain Initative: A National Public Health Roadmap to Maintaining Cognitive Health. Retrieved from Centers for Disease Control and Prevention Healthy Aging: https://www.cdc.gov/aging/healthybrain/resources.htm

National Institute on Aging. (2007, March). Growing Older in America: The Health and Retirement Study. Retrieved from National Institute on Aging Health and Aging: https://www.nia.nih.gov/health/publication/growing-older-america-health-and-retirement-study/preface

BRAIN HEALTH
7 Tips for Successful Aging

1. Successful Aging Starts at a Young Age...and Continues Through Old Age

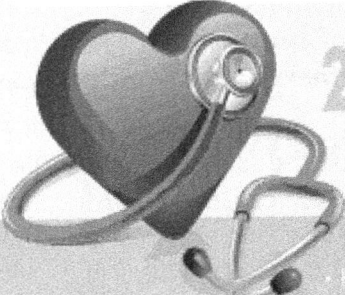

2. CONTROL RISK FACTORS for Alzheimer's Disease

- Diabetes · Obesity · Depression
- Heart Disease · High Blood Pressure

3. THE EVIL THREE: POOR DIET, INACTIVITY, SMOKING

ELIMINATING: Poor Diet, Inactivity, Smoking = 80% LESS Heart Disease, Stroke, Type 2 Diabetes = LESS ALZHEIMER'S DISEASE RISK

(Source: U.S. Centers for Disease Control and Prevention)

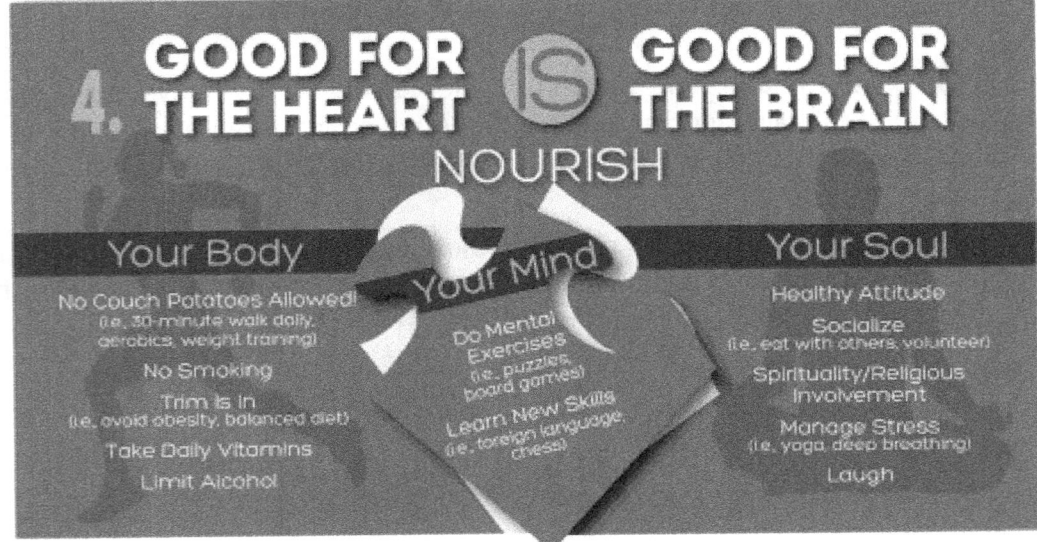

4. GOOD FOR THE HEART IS GOOD FOR THE BRAIN

NOURISH

Your Body
- No Couch Potatoes Allowed! (i.e. 30-minute walk daily, aerobics, weight training)
- No Smoking
- Trim Is In (i.e. avoid obesity, balanced diet)
- Take Daily Vitamins
- Limit Alcohol

Your Mind
- Do Mental Exercises (i.e. puzzles, board games)
- Learn New Skills (i.e. foreign language, chess)

Your Soul
- Healthy Attitude
- Socialize (i.e. eat with others, volunteer)
- Spirituality/Religious Involvement
- Manage Stress (i.e. yoga, deep breathing)
- Laugh

5. EAT SMART

Say YES to:
- Colorful, Dark-Skinned Fruits/Vegetables
  - Vitamin E Rich (i.e., blackberries, spinach)
  - Beta-Carotene Rich (i.e., broccoli, sweet potato)
- Whole Grains
- Omega-3 Fatty Acids (i.e., salmon, sardines)
- Antioxidants (i.e., blueberries, walnuts)

Say NO to:
- Red Meats
- Fried Foods
- Saturated Fats
- Processed Foods
- Salt
- Trans-Fatty Acids
- Added Sugars

6. SEE YOUR DOCTOR REGULARLY

Medicare Preventive and Screening Benefits:
- Cardiovascular Screenings
- Diabetes Screenings
- Depression Screenings
- Tobacco Use Cessation Counseling
- Medical Nutritional Therapy Services
- Detection of Cognitive Impairment

7. CAREGIVER CHECK-UP

Due to Behavioral/Cognitive Symptoms of a Loved One With Alzheimer's Disease, Caregivers (Most Commonly):

GIVE UP

Time With Friends/Family
- 43% behavioral
- 45% cognitive

Recreational Activities
- 39% behavioral
- 37% cognitive

SUFFER
- Fatigue
- Difficulty Sleeping
- Weight Gain
- Headaches
- Back Pain

MANAGE BY

Talking to Someone
- Friends
- Human Resources Dept.
- Clergy
- Healthcare Professionals

Doing Physical Activities

Doing Mental Activities

Getting Help
- Family
- Friends
- Volunteers

Going to House of Worship

Using Relaxation Techniques

©2013 Alzheimer's Foundation of America

Sanders-Brown Center on Aging

The Balm In Gilead acknowledges the University of Kentucky, Sanders-Brown Center on Aging as the developers of the original Memory Sunday, as a local initiative in the State of Kentucky.

The Sanders-Brown Center on Aging (SBCoA) was established in 1985, and received funding as one of the original 10 National Institutes of health Alzheimer's Disease Centers. Internationally acclaimed, the SBCoA is recognized for its contributions to the fight against brain diseases that are associate with aging.

As a global pioneer in Alzheimer's disease research, the Center has over thirty years of published work and 700 study volunteers (some with the disease and some without). These individuals are studied over time and plan to donate their brains upon death. The cutting-edge research focuses on identifying problems as early as possible, before memory loss develops, so that Alzheimer's disease can be prevented or delayed.

The ultimate goal of the Center on Aging is to catalyze innovative and outstanding brain research while ensuring a more rapid rate of progress toward new therapies to delay or prevent age-related brain diseases like Alzheimer's disease, so that our volunteers, patients and caregivers become beneficiaries of our advances in knowledge."

MEMORY SCREENING FACT SHEET

AFA's National Memory Screening Program (NMSP) provides free confidential memory screenings throughout the country on an ongoing basis. Since the inception of the program, more than 2.5 million people have been screened!

"At this time, there are types of memory problems that can be cured and other types that can be treated. The key is to recognize the problem, get screened and act on the results."

- J. Wesson Ashford, M.D., Ph.D. Chair, AFA's Memory Screening Advisory Board

WHAT ARE MEMORY SCREENINGS?

A memory screening is a simple and safe evaluation tool that checks memory and other thinking skills. It can indicate whether additional follow up with a qualified healthcare professional is needed.

- The screening takes approximately 10 minutes.
- Consists of a series of questions to gauge memory, language and thinking skills.
- Is conducted face-to-face and takes place in a private setting.
- Results are not a diagnosis, but a memory screening can suggest if someone should see a physician for a full evaluation.
- Results are completely confidential. The participant will receive the screening results to bring to a healthcare professional for follow-up and/or inclusion in medical files.

WHY SHOULD I BE SCREENED?

❖ **EARLY DETECTION**
Memory screenings are a significant first step toward finding out if a person may have a memory problem. Research suggests that screenings may detect cognitive impairment up to 18 years prior to clinical diagnosis of Alzheimer's disease or dementia.

❖ **SOME MEMORY PROBLEMS ARE TREATABLE**
Some memory problems can be readily treated, such as those caused by vitamin deficiencies or thyroid problems. Other memory problems might result from causes that are not currently reversible, such as Alzheimer's disease. The earlier the diagnosis, the easier it to treat or slow down the condition causing memory problems.

GET SCREENED. GET INFORMATION
WWW.NATIONALMEMORYSCREENING.ORG
866.232.8484

AFA's NMSP is made possible with a grant from the Edward N. and Della L. Thome Memorial Foundation, Bank of America, N.A., Trustee.

There Is a Balm in Gilead

By: African American Spiritual

Sometimes I feel discouraged and think my work's in vain,
But then the Holy Spirit revives my soul again.
There is a balm in Gilead to make the wounded whole;
There is a balm in Gilead to heal the sin sick soul.

If you cannot preach like Peter, if you cannot pray like Paul,
You can tell the love of Jesus and say, "He died for all."
There is a balm in Gilead to make the wounded whole;
There is a balm in Gilead to heal the sin sick soul.

Don't ever feel discouraged, for Jesus is your friend;
And if you lack for knowledge, He'll never refuse to lend.
There is a balm in Gilead to make the wounded whole;
There is a balm in Gilead to heal the sin sick soul.

About
The Balm In Gilead, Inc.

For almost three decades, The Balm In Gilead, Inc. builds and strengthens the capacity of African-American faith communities in the United States and in the United Republic of Tanzania (East Africa) to deliver programs and services that contribute to the elimination of health disparities. The organization develops educational and training programs specifically designed to establish sustainable, integrated systems of public health and faith principles, which helps to improve health outcomes of individuals living in urban, rural and remote communities.

The National Brain Health Center for African Americans and the Healthy Churches 2020 National Campaign are two unique programs of the Balm In Gilead, which delivers science-based, health awareness, understanding and interventions through the tenets of cultural competence to a broad spectrum of African Americans across the United States.

The Balm In Gilead, a not-for-profit, non-governmental organization, has developed an international reputation for providing insightful understanding of religious cultures, values and extraordinary abilities to build strong, trusted partnerships with faith communities throughout the world. By working with national, regional and local faith-based partners, we establish grass-root health delivery systems; and increase the number of individuals knowledgeable to lead in areas of health promotion, disease prevention, screening and disease management.

NOTES

www.ingramcontent.com/pod-product-compliance
Lightning Source LLC
Chambersburg PA
CBHW081636040426
42449CB00014B/3343